TRUCKS

GIANTS OF THE HIGHWAY

FOR KATHARINE McGONIGAL FLEMING

Thanks to Dwain Hurley, Charles Inman, and the family Jans—truckers and good folk all—and to Charles Jerkens and Randy Sallay at All Star Trucks for their patience and helpfulness.

—K. R.

First Aladdin Paperbacks edition December 2002
Text and illustrations copyright © 1999 by Ken Robbins

ALADDIN PAPERBACKS
An imprint of Simon & Schuster
Children's Publishing Division
1230 Avenue of the Americas
New York, NY 10020

Designed by Angela Carlino
The text of this book was set in Zurich Bold.
Printed in China
2 4 6 8 10 9 7 5 3 1

The Library of Congress has cataloged the hardcover edition as follows:
Robbins, Ken.
Trucks: giants of the highway/text and pictures by Ken Robbins.
p. cm.
Summary: Describes different kinds of tractor trailers, or big rigs, and the loads they haul.
ISBN 0-689-82664-8 (hc)
1. Tractor trailer combination—Juvenile literature. [1. Tractor trailers. 2. Trucks.] I. Title.
TL230.15.R63   1999   629.224—dc21
98-47640
ISBN 0-689-85217-7 (pbk.)

TRUCKS

GIANTS OF THE HIGHWAY

Text and pictures by Ken Robbins

ALADDIN PAPERBACKS

New York London Toronto Sydney Singapore

People call them big rigs. They are tractor-trailer trucks. You see them on the Interstate highways, gigantic, gleaming, brightly colored, loaded up with who knows what. It makes you wonder where they've been and where they're going as they rumble past like thunder on the road.

They are as much as seventy feet long and thirteen feet tall, and very, very powerful. These trucks can carry more than twenty tons of anything and everything that people use—from concrete blocks to running shoes.

There are two parts to these tractor-trailer rigs. The front part is the tractor. It holds the engine that pulls the entire load. It also holds the cabin, or cab, where the driver sits and drives.

And sometimes there's another compartment called a sleeper, right behind the cab, where the driver can lie down and nap for a while.

The semitrailer is the part that actually holds the load, but it has no engine to make it go. It has eight wheels that are all in the rear.

When the trailer is not connected to the tractor, the front of it rests on two posts called the landing gear.

Two wheels in the front of the tractor and eight wheels behind add up to ten. When those are combined with the eight wheels on the semitrailer, that makes the big rig an eighteen-wheeler.

The trailer may be one of several kinds. The flatbed trailer, for instance, has no top or sides. The load gets tied to the bottom, and that's where it rides.

The boxcar trailer is closed in on the sides and the top, and the doors in the back can be closed up and locked. Everything inside is safe from the weather. The inside can even be refrigerated.

The tanker is used for liquids and gasses—chemicals, gasoline, even milk—anything that can be spilled. Sometimes it carries a dangerous load—poisonous chemicals or stuff that could explode.

The dump truck has a bottom and sides, but it has no top. It carries things like gravel, dirt, or sand. The trailer tilts to dump the load.

There are other kinds of semitrailers, too—made to carry special loads of different sorts like automobiles or even horses.

Sometimes the tractor pulls more than one trailer. A truck that pulls two is called a tandem rig. They can't travel on most roads because they're too big, but you'll see them on the Interstate.

Sometimes even three trailers are hitched together.

Every day in America, hundreds of thousands of long-haul truckers drive up to warehouses, freight yards, or loading docks to pick up a load of something that's got to be taken from one place and moved to the next.

Perhaps the load must travel from Bangor, Maine, to Dallas, Texas, or from Macon, Georgia, to the Pacific Northwest.

Long-haul truckers are away from home many days at a time. It can be a lonely way of life. Some drivers take their families along.

Most drivers have to travel alone, but they can talk to one another as they drive along. They use a CB radio to call from truck to truck.

Some even have computers aboard to help them figure out where they are and where they need to go.

When truck drivers make a long-haul run, they don't have time to go shopping in stores or look around for a restaurant. So they look for a truck stop along the highway where they can park those big trucks at any time of the day or night.

There they can get whatever they need—fuel, spare parts, or something to eat.

Then it's back in the cab and on the road again for these long-distance, hard-driving women and men.